BODOLAND MOVEMENT (1986-2020) AND BEYOND

RITURAJ BASUMATARY

Contents

CHAPTER I

Introduction

The Bodos are one of the Indigenous People of North East India. In the heart of every social or political movement is the desire to bring some change in the pre-existing structure or ideology of society, and that is what Bodoland Movement aims to achieve. The Bodoland Movement strive to dismantle the existing geo-political setting in Assam and want a separate state out of it for the Bodo tribe of this area. The purpose of this article is to understand the need for this demand and to see how Bodoland Movement evolves over a period of time.

The foundation for Bodoland Movement was already laid in the British era when Britishers allowed the immigration of landless peasants from the densely populated bordering districts of Bengal (now Bangladesh) to the sparsely populated districts of the Brahmaputra valley of Assam which was dominated by the Bodo people. This process of migration was continued even after independence and in fact it blew out of proportion. The massive increase of migrant population put tremendous pressure on tribal land. This forced the tribal people to evict their land. In the post colonial period, tribal were forced to depend on the upper caste landlords ruling class. The tribal were also deprived of the benefit of industrialization and they remained at the level of peasant economy. The imposition of Assamese language as the official language of the state also fueled the resentment among Bodo people. All in all, the negligence shown by the government towards the welfare and protection of identity and culture of tribal people sowed the seed of Bodoland Movement.

CHAPTER II

Origin of the demand for separate state

The Tribal people of Assam had realized that they are being alienated on both economic and political platform and their culture, heritage and identity is facing threat under the umbrella of Assamese nationalism. The formation of All Assam Plains Tribal League (AAPTL) in 1933 and Bodo Sahitya Sabha (BSS) in 1952 shows Bodos quest for forming a socio-political identity. Platform for the Bodoland Movement was made with the formation of political organisations like the Plains Tribal Council of Assam (PTCA) and All Bodo Students' Union (ABSU) in 1967. PTCA raised the demand for the political autonomy of Bodos and this demand found expression with the idea of a separate union territory, namely Udayanchal comprising all the tribal areas of the north bank of the river Brahmaputra. Formation of PTCA was an important step in the evolution of Bodoland Movement, but PTCA gradually lost its relevance among common Bodos "because of their internecine conflict and their brief electoral alliances with the then Assam Government as PTCA had joined the short lived Janata Dal ministry led by Golap Borbora in 1978-79 and eventually moderated its demands to make the new administrative unit an autonomous region within Assam".

CHAPTER III

1st wave of Bodoland Movement

ABSU was formed in the same year as PTCA and it always played secondary role to PTCA. But soon ABSU realised that PTCA had failed to fulfill the aspirations of the Bodo people. With the election of Upendra Nath Brahma as its President in 1987, ABSU became the sole flag bearer of Bodoland Movement. Brahma decided to launch a democratic mass revolution on the principles of Gandhian non-violence aimed at formation of a separate state (Bodoland) by 1990 through a fifty-fifty division of Assam. ABSU submitted a memorandum to the Central Government on 22nd January 1987 demanding a separate state. They started mobilizing people against Assamese chauvinism and blamed Assamese people for the alienation of the tribal of Assam. An umbrella organization named Bodo People's Action Committee (BPAC) was formed to unite all sections of Bodo people irrespective of age and political affiliation. The ABSU and BPAC jointly organized a huge rally on 12th June 1987 at Judge's Field in Guwahati (Assam) where they coined the slogan "Divide Assam Fifty-Fifty". Soon they realized that their peaceful protests were not helping the cause and they revert to violent activities. Police were used to suppress the movement but it too failed in its effort.

CHAPTER IV

BAC Accord 1993

After many rounds of talk between Government and ABSU and other parties of interest, the Memorandum of Settlement (MOS) popularly known as Bodoland Accord was signed on 20th February 1993. The accord provided for a democratically elected Bodoland Autonomous Council (BAC) in the Northern Valley of the Brahmaputra river. It was not a separate state as envisioned by Bodos, but a administrative unit within Assam. The BAC Bill was introduced in the Assam State Assembly on 5 April 1993 and the Bill was enacted as Bodoland Autonomous Council Act, 1993.

CHAPTER V

2nd wave of Bodoland Movement

Formation of BAC provided some sort of autonomy to the Bodos within the state of Assam and it certainly slacked some tension, but it failed to fulfill the expectation of all section of Bodo people. In the backdrop of this discontent, two major militant organization came into existence, National Democratic Front of Bodoland (NDFB) demanding separate country and Bodo Liberation Tiger Force (BLTF) demanding separate state and these organisation rejected the BAC accord. Now these organisation was spearheading the Bodo cause, but with their violent method.

CHAPTER VI

BTC Accord 2003

In the mean time ABSU and BPAC also rejected BAC Accord in 1999 due to the various unresolved issues between government and BAC like demarcation of the boundaries of the BAC and they again launched a fresh movement this time demanding a complete autonomous separate state 'Bodoland'. However, they again end up with what they already had. On February 10, 2003 with the help of initiatives of ABSU, a memorandum of settlement was signed between Government of India, Assam Government and BLT. The main objectives of the agreement were to create an autonomous self-governing body to be known as Bodoland Territorial Council (BTC) within the state of Assam and to administer a territory spanning 3082 villages making four districts – Kokrajhar, Chirang, Baksa and Udalguri under the provisions of the Sixth Schedule of the Constitution of India, to abolish the Bodoland Accord of 1993, to fulfill economic, educational and linguistic aspirations and the preservation of land rights, socio-cultural and ethnic identity of the Bodos and to speed up the infrastructural development in the newly formed BTC area.

CHAPTER VII

3rd wave of Bodoland Movement

The All Bodo Students' Union (ABSU) restarted the third wave of Bodoland Movement from the year 2010 and the then UPA Government organized series of tripartite talk with the struggling organizations in the year 2013 and 2014 but didn't adopted any policy for permanent solution of the issue. On the other hand, the Union supported BJP led NDA in 2014 General Election as the BJP assured and included for solution of the Bodo issue as one of the point in their election manifesto (Additional).

A tripartite accord for final settlement of demands in Bodoland was signed on 27 January 2020 in New Delhi.

As per the accord, BTAD will now be named as Bodoland Territorial Region (BTR) and will have more administrative power.

CHAPTER VIII

BTR Accord 2020

The Tripartite Bodo Accord is a peace treaty signed on 27th January 2020 between the Assam State Government, Central Government and the National Democratic Front of Bodoland. The objective was to stop separatist demands from the Bodo-Kachari community and bring peace.

The Union Home Minister Amit Shah on 22nd March 2021 promised implementation of the clauses under the BTR Agreement within two-and-a-half years.

Key Highlights of the BTR Accord

- The Bodoland Territorial Area District (BTAD) was renamed Bodoland Territorial Region (BTR) on 27th January 2020 as a part of a peace treaty.
- The Bodo Peace Accord signed in 2020 is an extension of the existing agreement of 2003. The Bodo Accord attempts to strengthen the Bodo Territorial Region's legislative, administrative and financial status.
- Bodoland Territorial Region or BTR comprises Udalguri, Kokrajhar, Baksa and Chirang districts accounting for up to 10% of Assam's population and 11% of its area.
- Bodo-populated areas would aid efficient governance in Sixth Schedule administrative units in existing Bodoland Territorial Area Districts of Baksa, Kokrajhar, Chirang and Udalguri.
- The BTAD and area under the Sixth Schedule of the Constitution are exempt from the Citizenship

Amendment Act of 2019.

- This accord promises to form a committee including representatives from Bodoland Territorial Council and All Bodo Students Union to decide the inclusion and exclusion of new areas. This increased the number of assembly seats from 40 to 60.
- The Indian Central Government has sanctioned ?1500 crore as a Special Development Package for Bodo areas' development. This treaty has promised to pay ?5 lakh to families of deceased who participated in the Bodo movement.
- According to the Economics Times, the Government has already rehabilitated 2774 ex-cadres of the NDFB by 2021.
- Assam Chief Minister, Himanta Biswa Sarma, said that nearly 4949 landless families in BTR would receive land pattas to ensure exclusive land rights to residents.

CHAPTER IX

4th wave of Bodoland Movement

A new students' union - the Bodo National Students' Union (BoNSU) has revived the Bodoland statehood demand that is said to have ended with the signing of the Bodo Peace Accord in January 2020.

The union was formed in February 2022.

The students' union has revived the Bodoland statehood demand in Assam amidst the BJP's claim of resolving the Bodo problem through the signing of the historic Bodoland Territorial Region (BTR) pact.

In a memorandum submitted to Prime Minister Narendra Modi through the Kokrajhar district magistrate, the newly-formed Bodo National Students' Union (BoNSU) said the Centre had, over the past 30 years, signed three peace accords with the Bodo leadership but failed to fulfil the aspirations of the Bodos.

The students' body lamented that although the Bodos had struggled for long, their demands for socio-political, socio-cultural and economic development continued to remain unfulfilled.

BoNSU also said the Bodos' struggle for right to self-determination has its genesis in the British rule.

"As early as the 1930s, Gurudev Kalicharan Brahma, the then lone leader of the Bodos, had submitted a memorandum to the Simon Commission demanding a political setup for the indigenous and tribal people of Assam. However, his demand for political administration was ignored by the British Raj. Even in the post-independence era, such demands were not met by successive governments."

In 1967, the Bodos had demanded the creation of a Union Territory "Udayachal", by carving out an area of Assam from Sankosh to Sadiya along the foothills of Himalaya (Bhutan and Arunachal Pradesh), following the realisation that tribal blocks and belts notified by the British were being acquired by rich immigrant landlords.

Later in the 1980s, the All Bodo Students' Union (ABSU) had launched a mass movement. Almost around the same time, a section of the Bodo youth had taken up arms and formed an insurgent group, disillusioned by the government's apathy towards the Bodo movement.

Even as the struggle continued, the Assam government had formed the Bodoland Autonomous Council but the Bodos said it had failed to fulfil their socio-economic aspirations. Another accord, signed with insurgent group Bodo Liberation Tigers in 2003, had led to the creation of the autonomous Bodoland Territorial Council (BTC) but the movement continued. The BTR accord was signed in January 2020 with ABSU and four insurgent groups.

The BTC administers the four districts of Kokrajhar, Chirang, Baksa and Udalguri, falling under the BTR.

CHAPTER X

Conclusion

Bodoland Movement is the story of people's quest for self-determination, when people realizes that their culture, identity and anything they identify with is being threatened and overshadowed, there is a natural urge among the people to defend what is theirs, that is what happened with Bodo people. Since the colonial rule, there was a feeling of alienation among Bodos, but when this feeling remained same even after independence because of the ignorance of Government, people started organizing themselves in pursuit of political autonomy, which resulted in the formation of organisation like ABSU, PTCA, BLTF and many others. This struggle for self determination ended up with formation of Bodoland Territorial Region (for now). However, eleven state has gained statehood since 1967, when ABSU was formed, three from that same region (Manipur, Meghalaya and Mizoram) this raises intriguing questions. Even though the major phases of the Bodoland Movement was ended with the digning of the historic BTR Accord on 27th January 2020, but the movement for a separate state Bodoland still awaits a final resolution. The issue of a separate state Bodoland still continues to be a dominating issue in politics of Bodos.